this book is presented to:

_____

Bible Stories that end with a Hug!™

CREATED BY

Stephen Elkins

ILLUSTRATED BY

Simon Taylor-Kielty

TYNDALE KiDS

Tyndale House Publishers, Inc.

Carol Stream, Illinois

Visit Tyndale's website for kids at www.tyndale.com/kids.

TYNDALE is a registered trademark of Tyndale House Publishers, Inc.

The Tyndale Kids logo is a trademark of Tyndale House Publishers, Inc.

Bible Stories That End with a Hug!

Created by Stephen Elkins

Designed by Kimberly Sagmiller for Wonder Workshop and Jacqueline L. Nuñez

For manufacturing information regarding this product, please call 1-800-323-9400.

ISBN 978-1-4143-7543-4

Printed in China

18	17	16	15	14	13	12
7	6	5	4	3	2	1

table of contents

Dear Parents and Grandparents,

We all need love and affection in our lives, and what better way to say "I love you" than with a great big hug! *Bible Stories That End with a Hug!* will inspire your child to want to learn more about God and to seek and serve Him with a joyful heart!

In this book children will learn about God's love while growing closer to you. This collection of timeless Bible stories creates a delightful experience for you and your child. By using hugs to make your time together a special event, these stories foster a strong bond and help your child feel safe and loved.

As you read through these simple Bible lessons, watch as your child anticipates the hug waiting at the end of every story. Read these stories together and talk with your child about how to apply the lessons to daily life.

My prayer is that through this book you and your child will treasure the time you spend reading together, learning together, and sharing hug after hug! Everyone needs a hug, and everyone needs the Lord!

Stephen Elkins

♥ In the Beginning
Genesis 1

In the beginning God created the heavens and the earth.
(Genesis 1:1)

Imagine a time when there were no birds. There wasn't even a sky for them to fly in. In the beginning there was only God and a great big, empty universe. But that was about to change!

How did God change it?
God spoke, and everything came to be. "Let there be light," God said. And there was light. "Let there be fish and animals," He said. And they all came to be. God created all things, and they were good!

Did God create people, too?
Yes, He did!

God made whales and snails, hippos and hens. But then He made His greatest creation: people! And from the first man, Adam, and the first woman, Eve, came all the people of the earth, including you!

hug!
time

Give the one made by God . . . a great big hug!

♥ God Made People

Genesis 2:7-23

"I made you, and I will care for you."
(Isaiah 46:4)

The Bible tells us God created the heavens and the earth. He made the very first man and named him Adam. Then God made Eve, the first woman. Adam and Eve became God's very first family!

 What else did God do?

The Bible says that God made everything. He made the sun, moon, and stars, the animals that live on land, and all the fish that swim in the sea. There is no one like our God!

Did God make me, too?

Yes, He did!

He chose the color of your hair and skin. He formed your little nose, and your fingers and toes. He made you for His purpose and loves you just the way you are!

hug!
time

Give the one loved by God . . . a great big

hug!

♥ I Can Please the Lord
Genesis 4:1-5

Cain and Abel were sons of Adam and Eve. Together, they were the first family God created. But the two boys were very different. The oldest son, Cain, was a farmer. Abel took care of sheep. But in God's eyes, the difference was much greater than this.

♥ How were they different to God?

Abel did things that pleased God. Cain did not.
How did Abel please God? He loved God and obeyed
His commands.

♥ How can I please God?

By obeying His commands too!

God is pleased when we read the Bible and do the things
it says to do . . . like loving Him and being kind to others.
Let's all do things that please God!

hug!
time

Give the
one who
pleases the
Lord . . . a
great big

hug!

♥ Walking with God
Genesis 5:18-29; Jude 1:14-15

Enoch was the great-grandfather of Noah. The Bible says he walked with God for 365 years. Enoch loved God and kept His commands. Enoch spoke godly words to the people. When Enoch got old, he did not die. The Lord just took Enoch to heaven!

What did Enoch say that pleased God so much?

Enoch said, "The Lord is coming someday with thousands of angels. Love the Lord with all your heart, and stop doing bad things!" This was the message that pleased God so much.

Is what Enoch said still true today?

Yes, it is!

The Bible says that Jesus is coming back one day. And when He does come back, every eye will see Him. So, walk with God as Enoch did. Love God, and obey His commands!

hug! time

Give the one who walks with God . . . a great big hug!

They Laughed at Noah

Genesis 6–8

But the crowd laughed at Jesus.
(Luke 8:53)

Noah was a good man who loved God. One day God told Noah to build a giant boat called an ark. "Build it big enough to hold two of every kind of animal," God said.

18

What did Noah do?
He obeyed even though there wasn't a river or ocean for miles. And it had never rained before! When the people saw Noah's ark, they laughed and laughed! "Why are you building a boat out here, Noah? Are you crazy?"

 Will people laugh at me if I do what God says?
Maybe, but you should still obey God.

People laughed at Noah when he obeyed. They even laughed at Jesus! So don't be surprised if they laugh at you for obeying God's Word. Just remember . . . they stopped laughing at Noah when it started to rain!

hug!
time

Give
the one
who will
obey God
no matter
what . . . a
great big

hug!

♡ God Keeps His Promises

Genesis 18:1-15; 21:1-7

The LORD always keeps his promises.
(Psalm 145:13)

God promised Abraham and Sarah many children. But years passed, and they had none. Abraham and Sarah were now over 90 years old! They thought God had forgotten them.

 Did God forget his promise to Abraham and Sarah?
No! When Abraham was 99 years old, the Lord said, "Sarah will have a son." Sarah laughed because she was too old to have a baby! But our God always keeps His promises. Sarah named her baby boy Isaac.

 Has God made any promises to me?
Yes, He has!

There are lots of promises in the Bible. God promises to *answer your prayers*, *comfort you when you're sad*, and *forgive your sins*. Believe God! He always keeps His promises!

hug!
time

Give the one who believes God keeps His promises . . . a great big hug!

♥ Love, Listen, and Obey

Genesis 22

Honor your father and mother.
(Exodus 20:12)

Abraham loved God with all his heart. His son, Isaac, did too! Abraham obeyed when God asked him to go to Mount Moriah. And Isaac obeyed too when his father asked him to come.

💜 What happened on Mount Moriah?

Isaac honored his father by obeying him. He shared the workload by carrying the wood up the mountain. He never complained or questioned his father's decisions. He honored his father by listening and obeying.

💜 Should I honor my parents like that?

Yes, you should!

God's fifth commandment says to honor your parents. We can do this in three easy ways. First, *love* them. Second, *listen* to them. And third, *obey* them. To honor means to love, listen, and obey!

hug!
time

Give the one who honors their father and mother . . . a great big hug!

♥ Kindness Begins with Me

Genesis 24:1-27

Be kind to each other.
(Ephesians 4:32)

Abraham gave his most trusted servant a big job to do. "Go," Abraham said. "Find a wife for my son, Isaac. God will send His angel ahead of you to make sure you find the right girl."

Did the servant find the right girl?

He prayed, "God, please let the girl who offers me and my camels a drink be the right girl." Before he had finished praying, Rebekah came to the well. When she offered him a drink, he knew his prayer was answered!

What can I learn from Rebekah?

She was kind to others.

Rebekah showed her kindness by helping others. She shared with someone in need. So be like Rebekah and say, "Kindness begins with *me!*"

hug! time

Give the one who shows kindness . . . a great big *hug!*

♡ Angels on the Stairway

Genesis 28

> "I am with you, and I will protect you."
> (Genesis 28:15)

Jacob was traveling. When he had gone a long way, he stopped to rest for the night. As he slept, Jacob dreamed he saw a stairway to heaven. He saw God's angels walking up and down the stairs.

 What else did Jacob see?

He saw God standing at the top of the stairway. God said to Jacob, "I am with you, and I will protect you wherever you go." Jacob woke up and said, "God is in this place, but I didn't know it!"

 Is God with me, too?

Yes, God promised to be with you!

God has promised that He will be with you wherever you go. Whether you're going to school or the playground or somewhere far away, God is with you and will watch over you. And now you know it!

hug!
time

Give
the one
God
protects
. . . a
great big
hug!

The Coat of Many Colors

Genesis 37

God causes everything to work together for the good of those who love God.
(Romans 8:28)

28

Jacob had twelve sons. He gave his son Joseph a very special coat. It was a beautiful coat of many colors. Since Joseph's brothers did not have coats like that, they were very jealous. Then Joseph told his brothers about his dreams. They got angry and wanted to get rid of Joseph!

 What dreams did Joseph have?
Joseph had dreams about the future. He told his brothers that one day they would bow down to him. They got very angry and did a very mean thing. They sold Joseph to some traders going to Egypt.

 Did Joseph ever see his family again?
Not for many years!

But God never left Joseph. God used the bad things that happened to Joseph to save His people. If we love God, everything works together for good for us!

hug! time

Give the one who knows that everything works together for good . . . a great big hug!

♥ Joseph Does Not Get Even

Genesis 45:4-11; 50:19-21

See that no one pays back evil for evil, but always try to do good.
(1 Thessalonians 5:15)

Joseph was sold by his brothers to traders. As part of God's plan, he was taken to Egypt. Many years passed. Pharaoh, the king of Egypt, saw Joseph's wisdom. Joseph became a great leader in Egypt.

♥ What happened to his family?

There was no food in Israel. So Joseph's brothers went to Egypt to buy some. Who did they meet there? Their brother Joseph! God had sent Joseph to Egypt to save his family!

♥ Did Joseph get even?

No. Joseph's brothers had done an evil thing, but Joseph was good to them. Doing *good* is doing the things *God wants* us to do. Doing *evil* is doing the things *God doesn't want* us to do. Joseph did what was good in the sight of the Lord.

hug! time

♥

Give the one who will do good . . . a great big hug!

♥ Baby in a Basket
Exodus 1:6–2:10

God's people were living in Egypt as slaves. They had to serve a king who was very mean to them. As God's people grew in number, the king got scared. He worried that God's people might become stronger than his army.

What did the king do?

He said, "No more baby boys!" When a boy named Moses was born, his mother made a little basket to hide him. Then she put baby Moses in the basket to float in the Nile River. She would trust God to keep him safe.

 Did God keep him safe?

Yes, He did!

A princess found the baby and loved him. She named him Moses. That means "I drew him out of the water." Wherever you are, you can trust God to keep you safe!

hug!
time

Give the one God will keep safe . . . a great big hug!

♥ A Faithful Worker

Exodus 2:1-10

If you are faithful
in little things, you
will be faithful
in large ones.
(Luke 16:10)

34

Miriam was the older sister of baby Moses. When Moses was in danger, his mother made a basket and hid him inside. She put Moses in the basket and set him floating in the tall grass along the Nile River.

What did Miriam do?
Her job was to watch the basket. When Miriam saw a princess find the basket, she stepped forward. "Can I get a Hebrew woman to take care of the baby for you?" she asked. The princess agreed. Miriam had done her job well!

Miriam was faithful in little things, wasn't she?
Yes, she was!

When you are faithful with little jobs, like picking up your toys, God is pleased. It means you are growing up. Soon He will have more important things for you to do!

hug!
time

Give the one who is a faithful worker . . . a great big hug!

♥ God Will Fight for Me

Exodus 14

The LORD himself will fight for you. Just stay calm.
(Exodus 14:14)

God's people were finally free! Pharaoh had let them go. As they left Egypt, Pharaoh changed his mind. "What have we done?" he said. "If we don't have slaves, who will build our cities?" So his great army went to catch God's people and bring them back to Egypt.

How could God's people fight an army?
God's people were trapped at the Red Sea. Pharaoh's army was coming closer! Moses shouted, "The Lord will fight for you!" God parted the waters of the Red Sea. His people walked on dry ground to safety.

Will God fight for me?
Yes, He will!

Remember, Moses was not alone at the Red Sea. You are not alone either. God is with you, just like He was with Moses! Your God will fight for you!

hug! time

Give the one the Lord fights for . . . a great big hug!

♥ Breadflakes like Snowflakes

Exodus 16

God . . . will supply
all your needs.
(Philippians 4:19)

Moses led God's people through the desert. But soon they began to grumble against God. They were unhappy with the food. "We should have stayed in Egypt!" they said. "At least we didn't worry about starving!"

What did Moses do?
God told Moses that food would come. Every morning God would send white *breadflakes* like snowflakes to cover the ground. The breadflakes tasted like honey and were called manna. Every evening God would send meat for the people to eat. God would supply their needs!

Will God supply my needs too?
Yes, He will!

Remember the difference between *needs* and *wants*. *Needs* are things you must have to live, like food and shelter. *Wants* are everything else, like toys and candy. God has promised to meet your needs. The wants may have to wait!

Give the one whose needs are met by God . . . a great big

hug!

♥ What People Who Love Do

Exodus 20

Love fulfills the
requirements of
God's law.
(Romans 13:10)

God called Moses to Mount Sinai. There He gave Moses the 10 Commandments on stone tablets. These commandments would show God's people the right way to live. Together, they are a list of things that people who love God do and don't do.

❤ What does that mean?

People who *love* God obey Him. People who *love* God don't say bad things about Him. People who *love* others don't steal from them. People who *love* others don't lie to them.

❤ So God's law is all about love?

Yes, it is!

If we truly *love* God, we will obey Him and honor Him. If we truly love others, we will not hurt them or take what belongs to them. Why? Because we *love* them! People who love God and each other fulfill the law!

hug! time

❤ **Give the one who loves God and others . . . a great big** *hug!*

♥ Blessed to Be a Blessing

Numbers 22–23

"I will make you into a great nation. . . . You will be a blessing to others."

(Genesis 12:2)

An enemy from Moab had come to fight God's people. Their king wanted Balaam to do a bad thing. He offered Balaam lots of money to put a curse on God's people.

 What did Balaam do?

Balaam asked God for help. God sent an angel to block the road. Balaam couldn't see the angel, but his donkey did! When the donkey wouldn't move, Balaam hit the poor donkey. Then God let the donkey talk! "Why are you hitting me?" the donkey said. When Balaam saw the angel, he was sorry for hitting the donkey. The angel told Balaam to bless God's people instead of cursing them.

Did Balaam bless God's people?

Yes, he did!

Like Balaam, we can use our mouths to speak blessings or curses. If you are about to say an unkind word, stop! Use words wisely. Balaam learned to speak blessings. We are all blessed to be a blessing!

hug!
time

Give the one who is blessed to be a blessing . . . a great big hug!

♥ A God Who Saves

Joshua 2

Our God is a God
who saves!
(Psalm 68:20)

The city of Jericho stood between God's people and the Promised Land. Joshua sent two spies into the city. They stayed at Rahab's house. She helped them because she knew God would let them win the battle.

How did Rahab help them?
When the king's men came looking for the two spies, Rahab hid them on her roof. She said, "I have saved you. Now please save me and my family when the battle comes."

Were Rahab and her family saved?
Yes! Rahab was pulled out of *danger* and into *safety*.

When God saves, He pulls us out of death and into life . . . *eternal* life! That's why the Bible says our God is a God who saves.

hug!
time

Give the one who believes God saves . . . a great big hug!

♥ Do It God's Way

Joshua 6

The LORD was
with Joshua.
(Joshua 6:27)

Joshua knew what it meant to do things God's way. He had seen the Red Sea part and manna fall from heaven. So when God gave him the battle plan at Jericho, Joshua was surprised.

♥ What was the plan?

To bring down the walls of Jericho, God told Joshua to march around the city for seven days. Then the priests would blow their trumpets and the people would shout! This was not the usual battle plan!

♥ Did the walls fall?

Yes! When God's people shouted, the walls fell!

Like Joshua, we should listen to God. We can do that by reading the Bible. No matter how strange it may seem to others, God's way is always the right way.

hug!
time

♥

Give the one who does things God's way . . . a great big

hug!

♥ Deborah's Song of Praise

Judges 4–5

I will praise you with songs.

(Psalm 101:1)

God's people had done many bad things. So the Lord allowed a mean king to make them slaves. The people were sorry for what they had done. They cried out to God for help. He heard them and sent a wise leader named Deborah.

What made Deborah wise?
She listened to God and obeyed Him. She went with the army in battle. When God gave them victory, she sang this praise song: "I will sing to the Lord . . . and tell of the great things He has done!"

 Can I sing a praise song too?
Yes! Here's one you might already know.

"God is great. God is good.
And we thank Him for our food."

This song praises God for *who He is* and *what He has done*. Let's all praise the Lord!

hug! time

Give the one who praises the Lord . . . a great big *hug!*

♡ God Saw a Warrior

Judges 6:11-16

"I know the plans
I have for you,"
says the LORD.
(Jeremiah 29:11)

Gideon had a job to do. He was threshing the wheat to make grain. Gideon had to hide it from the enemy. As he was stacking the grain, an angel appeared and said, "Mighty hero, the Lord is with you!"

Was Gideon a mighty hero?
Gideon was a farmer, not a mighty hero or a warrior. He said, "How can the Lord be with me? All these bad things keep happening!" But the angel said, "Go, and win the battle for God's people. God will be with you!"

Does God have plans for me?
Yes, He does!

When everyone else looked at Gideon, they just saw a farmer. But God saw the mighty warrior he would be someday. I wonder what God sees when He looks at you.

hug!
time

Give the one God has plans for . . . a great big

hug!

♡ God Made Samson Strong

Judges 13–16

> God gives power to the weak and strength to the powerless.
> (Isaiah 40:29)

Manoah and his wife didn't have any children. They were surprised and happy when an angel appeared. "You will have a son," the angel said. "He will be a mighty man of God, strong and courageous!"

 Was a son born?

Yes, and they named the boy Samson. Samson grew to be the strongest man who ever lived! He defeated a lion with his bare hands, and a thousand men with only a donkey's jawbone. God had given Samson mighty strength.

Did Samson use his strength wisely?

No, he did not. God took away Samson's strength.

In his weakness, Samson asked God to make him strong one last time. God answered his prayer! When you feel weak, go to the One who gives strength. Go to God in prayer!

hug! time

Give the one whose strength comes from the Lord . . . a great big *hug!*

♥ "Wherever You Go, I Will Go."

The Book of Ruth

God has said, "I will never fail you. I will never abandon you."

(Hebrews 13:5)

Ruth loved her mother-in-law, Naomi. When Naomi's sons and husband died, she was alone. She decided to return to her hometown. Ruth knew the journey would be hard, but she wanted to go with Naomi!

♥ Wasn't Ruth afraid?

Ruth gave her time and effort to help someone she loved. She said to Naomi, "Wherever you go, I will go. Wherever you live, I will live." She would not leave Naomi alone. She would always stay with her!

♥ God makes that promise to us, too, doesn't He?

Yes, and He wants us to believe Him!

God is always with you, no matter where you go or how difficult things get. Other people might leave you, but God never will. He is faithful. God will never leave you alone.

hug!
time

Give the one who believes God is with them . . . a great big

hug!

♥ Sometimes We Wait

I Samuel I

Hannah was crying. She had asked the Lord many times for a child. But she still had none. Yet Hannah loved God and believed He could do anything! So again, she prayed.

What did Hannah pray?
She prayed, "If You will give me a son, I will give him back to You. He will serve You always." God answered her prayer! Hannah had a baby boy and named him Samuel. God's timing was perfect!

Will I have to wait for my prayers to be answered?
Sometimes, but be patient!

God answers *every* prayer. Sometimes He says, "Yes." Sometimes He says, "No." And sometimes He says, "Wait, and be patient." At just the right time, God will answer and give you just what you need!

hug! time

Give the one who waits on the Lord . . . a great big hug!

♥ "Speak, Lord. I Am Listening."

I Samuel 3

As a young boy, Samuel served God at the Temple. Eli was the priest. One night Samuel woke up. He heard a voice saying his name, "Samuel!" He thought it was Eli asking for him. So Samuel went to Eli and said, "I am here." But it was not Eli who called him!

♥ Who was it?

Samuel heard the voice again and again. Finally Eli figured out God was talking to Samuel. Eli told Samuel, "If you hear the voice again, say, 'Speak, Lord. Your servant is listening.'" That night God spoke to Samuel and gave him a special message!

♥ Will God speak to me?

Yes, God will speak through His Word.

We call the Bible "God's Word" because that's how God speaks to us. Everything you need to know about living for God is written there. When we listen to the Bible, we are listening to God! So read your Bible and say with Samuel, "Speak, Lord. Your servant is listening!"

hug!
time

Give the one who says, "I'm listening, Lord!" . . . a great big

hug!

♥ David and Goliath
1 Samuel 17

The name of the
LORD is a strong
fortress.
(Proverbs 18:10)

Goliath was a giant who stood nine feet tall! His army had come to fight God's people. Every day Goliath shouted mean things about God. But one day a shepherd boy named David heard Goliath making fun of God. David said, "I will go and fight him!"

💜 **How can a little shepherd boy win a fight with a giant warrior?**
David told Goliath, "Your strength is in your sword and spear. But my strength is the name of the Lord!" Then David put a stone in his slingshot and threw it at Goliath. David killed the giant! The *name* of the Lord gave him victory!

💜 **Is there really power in the *name* of the Lord?**
Yes, there is!

You have a name. God has a name too! It's Yahweh (yah-way). This name appears in the Bible more than six thousand times. David came in the *name* of the Lord—Yahweh! God gave David power to beat the giant!

hug! time

Give the one who knows the name of the Lord . . . a great big hug!

61

♥ The Two *T*'s of Friendship

1 Samuel 18:1-4

A real friend sticks closer than a brother.
(Proverbs 18:24)

David won the battle against the giant soldier, Goliath. The king wanted to meet David. He invited David to serve at the palace. There David met Jonathan, the king's son. Jonathan and David became best friends!

What made them such good friends?
David and Jonathan spent **T**ime together, and they **T**rusted each other. Jonathan gave David his robe, his sword, his belt, and his bow and arrows. These gifts showed his friendship. David and Jonathan made a promise to always help each other.

Do all friendships need Time and Trust?
Yes, they do.

A real friend is someone who spends **T**ime getting to know you. A friend is also someone you can always **T**rust to help you. **T**rust and **T**ime are the two *T*'s of friendship!

hug!
time

Give the one who knows the two *T*'s of friendship . . . a great big

hug!

The Peacemaker

I Samuel 25

God blesses those who work for peace.
(Matthew 5:9)

Abigail was a wise, nice woman. But her husband was mean. He said unkind things to King David. That made David angry. But Abigail was a peacemaker. She knew what to do! She asked David to forgive her foolish husband. Then she gave David a peace offering of good food.

 Did David accept her peace offering?
Yes! David knew Abigail wanted peace more than anything. So David said, "Go home in peace, Abigail. I forgive your husband." Abigail was indeed a peacemaker!

 **Can I be a peacemaker too?**
Yes, you can!

Sometimes you may not know what to say to get along with others. But you can always pray. God will help you to think, act, and speak like a peacemaker!

hug!
time

Give
the one
who is a
peacemaker
. . . a
great big
hug!

♥ Ravens Bring Elijah Food

1 Kings 17:2-6

God . . . will certainly care for you. . . . So don't worry.

(Matthew 6:30-31)

Elijah was in danger. The Lord told Elijah, "Leave here. Go hide in a safe place near the Kerith Brook. I will give you water to drink from the brook. And ravens will bring you food to eat." So Elijah obeyed God.

❤ Did the ravens really bring food to Elijah?

Yes, they did! Every morning and every evening, black birds called ravens brought Elijah bread and meat. And Elijah drank the water from the brook. God supplied all Elijah's needs.

❤ Will God meet my needs too?

Yes, God has promised to take care of you and meet your needs!

Jesus said not to worry about things we need because God will supply them. God knows what we need before we even ask! You can trust God to take care of your needs.

hug! time

Give the one whose needs are met . . . a great big **hug!**

♡ Listen and Obey

2 Kings 5:1-14

If they listen and
obey God, they will
be blessed.
(Job 36:11)

There is good news and bad news in Naaman's story. First the good news: He was a great soldier! All the people loved Naaman, and God helped him win many battles.

 What's the bad news?
Naaman had a terrible skin disease called leprosy. A Hebrew servant girl told Naaman to go see Elisha to be healed. Elisha told Naaman, "Go wash in the Jordan River seven times." Naaman was cured because he listened and obeyed!

How do we listen to and obey God today?
We open the Bible and read the words of God.

Reading the Bible is like listening to God Himself. He inspired the words, so we can trust them to be true. You can listen and obey by reading your Bible.

hug!
time

Give the one who listens to God and obeys . . . a great big

hug!

♡ An Answered Prayer
1 Chronicles 4:9-10

"Oh, that you would bless me."
(1 Chronicles 4:10)

Jabez loved God and wanted others to love Him too. So Jabez prayed and asked the Lord for something very special. He asked God to bless him, so that he could bless others.

♥ What did Jabez ask for?

Jabez prayed for three important things. First, he prayed that God would bless him and give him more land. Then he asked God to be with him. Finally he asked God to keep him safe and healthy. What a wonderful prayer!

♥ Did God answer Jabez's prayer?

The Bible says God's answer was, "Yes!"

God said, "Yes, I will bless you and give you more land! Yes, I will be with you. Yes, I will keep you safe and healthy." You can ask God for the same things. Pray that God will bless you, too!

hug!
time

Give the one who prays for God's blessing . . . a great big hug!

♥ Honor God with L-O-V-E

2 Chronicles 34

Don't . . . forget your Creator. Honor him in your youth.
(Ecclesiastes 12:1)

Josiah was only eight years old, but he was *king* of God's people! Can an eight-year-old boy do the right things that honor God? Josiah could! Because of his **L-O-V-E**, God was pleased with him.

♥ **What is L-O-V-E?**
That's how we honor God. Josiah **L**oved God and worshiped only Him. He **O**beyed God when they found the lost Book of God's Law. Josiah **V**owed a promise to serve God. Then he **E**ncouraged his people to do the same!

♥ **Should I promise to L-O-V-E God too?**
Yes, you should!

No matter how young or old you are, you should always honor God with **L-O-V-E**. **L**ove God. **O**bey God. **V**ow to serve God. **E**ncourage others to serve Him too! If you do these things, God will be honored!

hug! time

♥

Give the one who honors God with L-O-V-E . . . a great big hug!

This Wall Begins with Prayer
The Book of Nehemiah

When Nehemiah heard the news, he cried out loud. The wall of Jerusalem was torn down, and the gates were burned! That made Nehemiah very sad. He wanted to rebuild the wall. But first he had to get the king's permission to do this.

What did Nehemiah do?

Before starting this big job, Nehemiah prayed. He asked God to help him and to bless the work he was going to do. Nehemiah prayed, and God gave him what he needed to rebuild the wall!

Should I pray before I start a big job?

Yes! Whether big or small, every job should begin with prayer.

Ask God to be your helper. Ask Him for the strength and wisdom to finish the job. God helped Nehemiah rebuild the wall. He will help you with your jobs too!

hug!
time

Give the one who prays before the job begins . . . a great big

hug!

♥ A Brave Witness
The Book of Esther

Wait patiently for the LORD. Be brave.
(Psalm 27:14)

Queen Esther was a beautiful woman of God. She found out that a terrible man named Haman wanted to get rid of all God's people, the Jews. Only Queen Esther could stop Haman. But she would have to go see the king.

♥ Was Esther allowed to see the king?
No. But she said, "Even if he kills me, I will go to the king." She asked God's people to fast for three days. Then Esther told the king about Haman's evil plan. Because of Esther's bravery, God's people were saved!

♥ Can I be a brave witness too?
Yes, you can!

Esther was very brave to speak to the king and save God's people. You must be brave too! Tell your friends and family about Jesus. Be a brave witness, and God will be pleased!

hug! time

♥

Give the one who is a brave witness . . . a great big hug!

Comfort My People

The Book of Job

He comforts us . . . so that we can comfort others.
(2 Corinthians 1:4)

God was pleased with Job and blessed him in every way. One day Satan came before God and said, "Job loves you because you give him good things. If you take them away, he won't love you anymore."

💜 **What did God do?**
He allowed Satan to take Job's health and wealth away. Job lost his family and his money, and he got very sick. Job's friends came to comfort him. They sat with Job for seven whole days without saying a word.

💜 **Is it okay to be quiet when others are hurting?**
Yes, it is.

When we don't know what to say, just being there says it all! It says you care enough to come. God is pleased when we comfort the hurting and show them love.

Give
the one
who will
comfort
the hurting
. . . a
great big
hug!

♥ David the Shepherd Boy

Psalm 23

David was a shepherd who took good care of his sheep. A shepherd *knows* the needs of his sheep. He *shows* his sheep where they can find food and water. And he *grows* his sheep so they become healthy and strong.

❤️ **Do shepherds watch their sheep day and night?**
Yes, they do. At night as David watched his sheep, he would write poems to God called psalms. He wrote, "The Lord is *my* Shepherd." That means the Lord *knows* him, the Lord *shows* him the way, and the Lord *grows* him by keeping him safe and strong!

❤️ **Is the Lord my Shepherd too?**
Yes, He is!

The Lord is your Shepherd. He watches over you day and night. He *knows* you, *shows* you, and *grows* you as His little lamb!

hug! time

❤️

Give the one God watches over . . . a great big hug!

81

♥ Jesus Is Coming!

Isaiah 62:11

"Look, your Savior is coming."
(Isaiah 62:11)

Isaiah was a great messenger of God called a prophet. He was blessed with a special gift. God let Isaiah see things that would happen in the future. Isaiah would write down what God told him.

What did Isaiah write down about the future?
Isaiah wrote that Jesus was coming! He wrote this 700 years before Jesus was born! Isaiah also said Jesus would perform miracles and would die for our sins. Isaiah was right! Jesus did come . . . and very soon, He's coming again!

Does anyone know when Jesus is coming again?
Only God, our heavenly Father, knows.

Jesus said that only the Father knows when He is coming again. But before Jesus comes, people will say, "He's not coming!" We have to remember what Isaiah wrote: "Look, your Savior *is* coming!"

hug!
time

Give the one who believes Jesus is coming soon . . . a great big

hug!

♥ Showers of Blessing

Ezekiel 33–34

"There will be showers of blessing."
(Ezekiel 34:26)

God made a promise to Ezekiel. God would be a Shepherd to all who love Him. So God said, "I will look after them and keep them safe. I will watch over them, and there will be showers of blessing!"

♥ What is a blessing?

Blessings are God's way of showing He is pleased. He sends good things to those who love and obey Him. A "shower of blessing" means too many blessings to count . . . more than the raindrops falling from the sky!

♥ Has God ever blessed me?

Yes, He has!

God blesses us with things like family, friends, clothes, and food. But the greatest blessing of all is Jesus. Because of Him, we will someday share the blessing of heaven!

hug!
time

Give the one who is showered with blessings . . . a great big hug!

♥ Let's Worship the Lord

Daniel 3

Shadrach, Meshach, and Abednego wanted to please God. So when an evil king told them to worship an idol, they refused! They told the king they would only *worship* the one true God.

Was the king angry with them?

Very angry! To punish them, the king threw them into a flaming furnace! But they weren't trying to win the king's approval . . . only God's. They knew He was the only One worthy of worship. God was pleased. He saved them from the flaming furnace!

What does it mean to *worship*?

We worship what is most important to us.

God is still the only One worthy of our worship. Worship means to love someone or something more than anything else. God wants to be that Someone. He wants us to worship Him and Him alone.

hug!
time

Give the
one who
worships
God
alone . . . a
great big
hug!

♥ Daniel in the Lions' Den

Daniel 6

Never stop praying.
(1 Thessalonians 5:17)

The men Daniel commanded did not love God. They were angry that Daniel prayed three times a day. So they tricked the king into passing an evil law. The law said, "Anyone who prays to God will be punished!"

❤️ **Did Daniel stop praying?**

No! Daniel loved God with all his heart. He couldn't stop talking to the God he loved! When the king found out Daniel had broken the law, he threw Daniel into a den of hungry lions! What do you think Daniel did? He prayed! And God kept him safe.

❤️ **Can I learn to pray like Daniel did?**

Yes, you can!

The Bible teaches that we should never stop praying. When good things are happening, pray to God and thank Him! When things are hard, pray and ask God for help. No matter what is happening, pray!

hug! time

❤️

Give the one who is learning to always pray . . . a great big hug!

Obey the First Time!

The Book of Jonah

"I cried out to the LORD in my great trouble, and he answered me."
(Jonah 2:2)

Our troubles usually begin when our obedience ends. God told Jonah to go to Ninevah. But Jonah didn't want to go there. So he got on a ship going the other way. Jonah chose to disobey the Lord.

 What happened next?
God sent a terrible storm. Jonah found himself sinking deep in the waves. Then, *gulp!* He was swallowed by a giant fish. Jonah prayed and asked God to help him!

Should I pray when I'm in trouble?
Yes, you should!

Even though Jonah had disobeyed, God heard his prayer and forgave him. God used Jonah's trouble to teach a great lesson. Obey God the *first* time.

hug! time

Give the one who obeys God the *first* time . . . a great big hug!

♥ The Messiah in a Manger

Luke 2

When Jesus was born, He didn't have a nice crib to sleep in. So His mother, Mary, put baby Jesus in a wooden box called a manger. An angel came to tell some shepherds Jesus was born. The angel said, "You will find the **Messiah** sleeping in a manger!" It was a sign that Jesus was sent from God.

What does *Messiah* mean?
Messiah means two things: **anointed**
and **appointed**. *Anointed* means "to be
covered." *Appointed* means "to be given a job."
Jesus is our Messiah. He was *anointed* and
appointed by God to save us from our sins!

 Is Jesus the Messiah?
Yes, He's the Messiah in a manger!

Jesus was *anointed* and *appointed* to save God's people.
The name *Jesus* means "God saves." Jesus was
covered by God's love and
given the job of salvation.
Only He could do that!

hug!
time

Give the
one who
knows what
Messiah
means . . . a
great big

hug!

♥ Tell about the Savior
Luke 2:36-38

"Go into all the world and preach the Good News to everyone."
(Mark 16:15)

Anna was an old woman who loved God. She spent all her time serving in the Temple. There she worshiped and prayed to God. When Jesus was only eight days old, Mary and Joseph brought Him to the Temple. Anna was so excited to see baby Jesus! She thanked God for the Christ child.

♥ What did Anna do next?

Though Anna was very old, she told everyone about Jesus. She would say, "The Promised One has come! I have seen Him!" Anna wanted everyone to know that Jesus the Savior had come!

♥ Should I tell others about Jesus too?

Yes, you should!

The Bible says that we should all *go and tell* others about Jesus . . . in our town, our state, our country, and all over the world! You can start with your own family and friends. *Go and tell* them about Jesus today!

hug!
time

♥

Give the one who will *go and tell* about Jesus . . . a great big

hug!

♥ Growing by Knowing

Luke 2:41-52

Jesus grew in wisdom and in stature and in favor with God and all the people.
(Luke 2:52)

When Jesus was a boy, what was He like? Did He like to sing or draw or read? Did He play with friends or chase butterflies? We don't know for sure. But we do know Jesus loved to go to church (called the Temple) to talk about God, His Heavenly Father.

 What does the Bible tell us about Jesus as a boy?
When Jesus was 12, His family took Him to the Temple. For three days Jesus listened to the teachers there and asked questions. He was *growing by knowing*. This pleased God!

How can I start *growing by knowing*?
Be like Jesus!

Jesus loved to go to church. It's a great place to listen to teachers and ask questions about the Bible. So be like Jesus. Start *growing by knowing* . . . and learning more about God!

hug!
time

Give the one who is *growing by knowing* God . . . a great big

hug!

♥ John the Baptist

Matthew 3

John the Baptist stood in the Jordan River. There he baptized people who wanted God to forgive their *sins*. Baptism is a way of saying, "I am sorry for my *sins*." One day Jesus came to be baptized. John said, "You should baptize me, Jesus."

💜 **Why didn't John want to baptize Jesus?**
John knew that Jesus was perfect—*He had no sin!* But Jesus said that He must be baptized because one day He would take your sin, my sin, and everyone's sin upon Himself. So John baptized Jesus that day.

💜 **Should I be baptized too?**
Baptism is a sign on the outside of a change on the inside.

If you believe Jesus has taken your sins away, you may want to be baptized to show your love for Jesus. Do it by faith because God has asked you to do it. Obey and be baptized, just like Jesus!

hug! time

Give the one who will obey God and be baptized . . . a great big hug!

♥ Fishing for People

Matthew 4:18-22

"Come, follow me."
(Matthew 4:19)

Jesus was walking by the Sea of Galilee. There He saw a fisherman named Peter throwing his net into the water. Jesus shouted, "Come, follow me, and I will show you how to fish for *people*!"

What did Peter do?

Right away, Peter dropped his net and followed Jesus. Peter walked with Jesus all the days of his life. He became a great fisher of people by telling them about Jesus.

 Can I "fish for people" too?

Yes, you can!

To catch fish, you must go where the fish are. When you fish for people, you go to them and tell them about God's love. Be a fisherman for Jesus!

hug!
time

Give the one who is a "fisher of people" . . . a great big

hug!

♥ Practice What Jesus Preached

Matthew 5–7

He began to
teach them.
(Matthew 5:2)

Jesus sat on a mountainside to teach His followers. He taught that the Kingdom of God belongs to those who live to honor Him. The people were amazed by His teaching.

💜 **What else did Jesus teach?**
He taught the people to love each other, forgive those who do wrong, and give to those in need. He even taught them how to pray. It was the greatest sermon ever!

💜 **Can we do the things Jesus taught?**
Yes, we can!

The last words of this sermon say, "Anyone who hears and obeys my words is *wise*. But those who hear and do not obey are foolish." Be wise, and practice what Jesus preached!

hug!
time

Give the one who will practice what Jesus preached . . . a great big hug!

♥ Life-Changers!
Matthew 5:13-16

"No one lights a lamp
and then puts it
under a basket."
(Matthew 5:15)

104

Jesus said, "You are the *salt* of the earth. Don't lose your saltiness. You are the *light* of the world. Don't hide your light under a basket!"

 What did Jesus mean?
Jesus wanted His followers to be life-changers. That's why He used the examples of salt and light. Salt changes the flavor of food. Light changes a dark room and makes it bright.

Can I be a life-changer for Jesus?
Yes! Just be salt and light to everyone you meet!

Your words can change a life. Tell people about Jesus. Your actions can make a difference. Be kind and loving. That's the kind of salt and light Jesus is looking for!

hug! time

Give the one who shines for Jesus . . . a great big hug!

♥ He Already Knows!

Matthew 6:1-18

"Your Father knows exactly what you need even before you ask him!"
(Matthew 6:8)

Jesus said there are right reasons and wrong reasons to pray and give. It's good to pray to God and to give to the poor. But some people do these good things for the *wrong* reasons. They don't want others to know how good *God* is. They just want to show how good *they* are!

 What is the right reason to pray?

Those who love God and want to spend time with Him pray for the right reasons. They believe that He already knows what's best for them before they even ask. When we talk to God, we should pray like Jesus did:

> "Our Father in heaven, may Your name be kept holy. May Your Kingdom come soon. May Your will be done on earth, as it is in heaven. Give us today the food we need, and forgive us our sins, as we have forgiven those who sin against us. And don't let us yield to temptation, but rescue us from the evil one."

Does God already know what I need?

Yes, He does!

Even before the sun comes up, God already knows your needs for tomorrow . . . *and* He has promised to supply every single one. Our Father in heaven is an awesome God!

hug! time

Give the one who prays and trusts God with their tomorrow . . . a great big hug!

♥ My First and Best Love

Matthew 6:19-34

"Seek the Kingdom of God above all else, and live righteously, and he will give you everything you need."

(Matthew 6:33)

When we give our heart to Jesus, He becomes our *first and best love*. We cannot have two *first loves*. Jesus said we cannot serve both God and money. But He told us not to worry because God will take care of us. Make God your *first love*!

♥ How do I stop worrying?

When you start trusting God, you will stop worrying! "Look at the sparrows," Jesus said. "They don't worry, but God takes care of them. Seek God first, and don't worry about tomorrow."

♥ Can God be my *first and best love*?

Yes, He can!

If you seek God first above all else, if you love Him first above all others, He will become your first love! Make God your first and best love, and He will give you everything you need!

hug! time

Give the one whose *first and best love* is God . . . a great big

hug!

♥ Keep on Knocking

Matthew 7:7-11

> "Keep on knocking, and the door will be opened to you."
>
> (Matthew 7:7)

Jesus had a lesson for quitters. He said we should never quit *asking* in prayer. Never quit *seeking* God's truth. Never quit *knocking* on doors where we can serve God. Never give up! Look up, and keep praying!

 Why do we have to keep asking? Why doesn't God answer our prayers right away?
Sometimes God doesn't answer our prayers because it isn't the right time yet. God loves giving good gifts to His children. So *keep asking* in prayer until the answer comes. *Keep seeking* God, and *keep knocking* until God opens the door.

 Will God give good gifts to me?
Yes, He will!

If you *keep asking*, He promises to give. If you *keep seeking*, God promises you'll find what you're looking for. If you *keep knocking*, He will open doors where you can serve Him.

hug! time

Give the one who keeps asking, seeking, and knocking . . . a great big hug!

♥ Jesus Is Your Strong Rock!

Matthew 7:24-27

The LORD is my rock.
(Psalm 18:2)

Jesus once told the story of the wise and foolish builders. The wise man built his house on a rock. When the storm came, the house did not fall. It was built on a big, strong rock that couldn't be moved.

♥ What did the foolish builder do?

He built his house on the sand. The sand was not strong like the rock was. When the storm came, the house built on sand fell down! Jesus told this story to teach us to build our lives on a firm foundation.

♥ How can I be a wise builder?

Trust Jesus, and build your life on Him. He is your strong rock!

Put the words of Jesus into practice. Build on the firm foundation of His Word, the Bible. When trouble comes, you will stand firm. You will be safe because your life is built on the Rock called Jesus! Choose to be wise and follow Him.

hug! time

Give the one who is building on the Rock called Jesus . . . a great big hug!

♡ Jesus Calms the Storm
Matthew 8:23-27

Even the wind and waves obey him!
(Matthew 8:27)

114

Jesus and His disciples got into a boat and started to cross a lake. Suddenly, a terrible storm came. The waves were so high that they crashed onto the deck of the boat!

 What did Jesus do?
Jesus was asleep. But His disciples were very scared! They cried out to Jesus, "Save us!" Jesus got up and told the storm, "Be still!" Right away, the wind and waves obeyed Him. Everything was calm.

 Do the wind and waves *still* obey Jesus?
Yes, they do!

Whenever you are afraid, it's good to know you can call on Jesus for help. He will either calm the storm or calm you until the storm passes. You don't have to be afraid, because the wind and waves still obey Him!

hug!
time

Give
the one
who calls on
Jesus in the
storm . . . a
great big
hug!

♥ Growing a Giant Faith

Matthew 17:14-20

Faith is the confidence that what we hope for will actually happen; it gives us assurance about things we cannot see.

(Hebrews 11:1)

A man brought his sick boy to Jesus' disciples. They tried to heal the boy, but they could not. "Why, Jesus?" the disciples asked. Jesus said, "Your faith isn't strong enough!"

What did Jesus mean?

Faith is a growing thing, like a plant. A big tree can grow from a little seed. Jesus said, "If your faith was the size of a tiny mustard seed, you could move mountains. Nothing would be impossible for you to do." If you use your faith, it will grow bigger and stronger!

How do I grow my faith?

By obeying God's Word!

We never know what will happen when we obey, but God knows. If the Bible says, "Don't tell lies," use your faith to tell the truth. If the Bible says, "Love others," use your faith to be nice and to share. Do what the Bible says . . . and watch your faith grow!

hug! time

Give the one whose faith is growing like a mustard seed . . . a great big *hug!*

♥ The Little Lost Lamb

Matthew 18:12-14

"It is not my heavenly Father's will that even one of these little ones should perish."
(Matthew 18:14)

Jesus told a story to show that God's love is big enough for everyone. He said, "A shepherd had 100 sheep. But one sheep walked away and got lost."

What did the good shepherd do?

"He went to find the lost sheep! He left the 99 sheep who were safe to look for the one little lost lamb. And when he found it, he was so happy! Just like the shepherd, God wants everyone to be safe with Him."

Will God look for me if I get lost?

Yes! He sent Jesus to find everyone who is lost and to save them.

Jesus' story about the lost sheep is really about God's love. God doesn't want anyone to miss heaven. He loves each one of His "little lambs." Jesus is the Good Shepherd who looks for lost sheep!

hug!
time

Give the little lamb Jesus loves . . . a great big hug!

♥ Friends of Faith

Mark 2:1-12

A friend is
always loyal.
(Proverbs 17:17)

The house was crowded with lots of people. They all wanted to hear Jesus teach the Good News of God's love. Suddenly, pieces of the ceiling started falling. Everyone looked up. Four men were tearing a hole in the roof!

 What was happening?
The four men knew Jesus could heal their sick friend. But they couldn't get through the crowd. So they made a hole in the roof and lowered their friend down, right in front of Jesus. Jesus healed the sick man because he had *friends of faith*.

Can I be a *friend of faith* like that?
Yes, you can!

Friends of faith are very special people. They don't let anything keep them from bringing their friends to Jesus. Be a friend of faith to someone you know!

hug!
time

Give the one who is a *friend of faith* . . . a great big hug!

♥ A Little Boy's Lunch

John 6:1-13

Share with those in need.
(Hebrews 13:16)

Five thousand people had gathered to listen to Jesus. It was getting late, and everyone was hungry. A little boy was willing to share his lunch. But it was only five small loaves of bread and two fish.

 What did Jesus do?
Jesus took the little boy's lunch, blessed it, and thanked God for it. Then He broke the bread and the fish into pieces and gave them to the people. Everyone ate until they were full. There were 12 baskets of food left over!

Can I share what I have with Jesus?
Yes, you can!

We can keep what we have, or we can give it to Jesus. Like the loaves and fish, a little bit blessed by Jesus becomes a whole lot!

hug!
time

Give the one who shares with Jesus . . . a great big

hug!

♥ **Jesus Loves Children!**

Mark 10:13-16

"Let the children come to me."

(Mark 10:14)

Jesus loves children! Some parents brought their children to Jesus so He could pray for them. But Jesus' disciples told them to go away. They thought Jesus only had time for *big people*, not for children.

♥ What did Jesus do?

He got angry at His disciples. Jesus said, "Let the children come to Me. God's Kingdom belongs to people who are like these children." Then Jesus hugged the children and prayed for God to bless them.

♥ What lesson was Jesus teaching?

Depend on God for everything.

Children don't worry about jobs or money. They depend on loving parents to meet their needs. Our heavenly Father wants us to depend on Him like that! No matter how young or old we are, we should always depend on God.

hug! time

♥ Give the one who depends on the Lord . . . a great big hug!

♥ Calling Doctor Jesus!

Luke 5:27-32

CLOSED FOR BUSINESS

Matthew was a busy tax collector. Then Jesus came and said, "Follow me." Right away, Matthew walked away from his tax business to become a disciple of Jesus. Later, Matthew had a big party at his house to honor Jesus.

❤ What happened next?

Many tax collectors came. The church leaders asked Jesus, "Why do You eat with these bad people?" Jesus answered, "All of these bad people are sick. They need forgiveness." Jesus is like a doctor who can heal our hearts and make us healthy.

❤ Do we still need Doctor Jesus today?

Yes, we do!

Only Jesus can heal our sinful hearts. To Jesus, "sin" and "sickness" mean the same thing. So whether Jesus heals our sickness or forgives our sin, He is still Doctor Jesus!

hug! time

❤

Give the one who is healed by Doctor Jesus . . . a great big hug!

♥ Go and Do

Luke 10:25-37

One day a man asked Jesus a tricky question: "Who is my neighbor?" Jesus answered with a story about a "**go** and **do**" person. Jesus said, "A man had been beaten up, robbed, and left by the side of a road. Then three men came along."

What did the men do?

Two men passed by the hurt man. But the third man stopped and helped him. Then Jesus asked, "Which of the three was a good neighbor?" The man said, "The one who helped." Jesus said, "Yes. **Go** and **do** the same thing."

 What should I go and do?

Help others!

As you **go** through each day, you should **do** kind things for others. If you see someone with a need, help that person. When you do, you become a good neighbor! And that's exactly what Jesus wants you to be!

hug! time

Give the one who is a good neighbor . . . a great big hug!

♥ Mary and Martha
Luke 10:38-42

Mary and Martha were sisters who both loved the Lord. One day Jesus came to their house! Martha kept busy cooking and cleaning. Mary sat at Jesus' feet and listened carefully to every word He said.

Did Martha do all the work?

Yes, and she got upset. "Tell Mary to help me!" she said. Jesus replied, "Martha, your sister is doing the right thing. It's good to work hard, but it's even better to learn about the Kingdom of God."

 Should we be like Mary or Martha?

We can be like both of them. There is a time to *work* like Martha and a time to *listen* like Mary.

If your *work* keeps you from *listening* to God, you may need to work a little less and listen a little more. Just remember to listen like Mary and work like Martha!

hug!
time

Give the one who listens like Mary and works like Martha . . . a great big

hug!

131

♥ Thank God Every Day

Luke 17:11-19

Give thanks to the LORD for he is good!

(Psalm 136:1)

Jesus said that faith can move a mountain. It can also remove (or take away) a mountain of misery and bring great joy. One day Jesus met 10 men who had leprosy, a terrible skin disease. They shouted, "Jesus, heal us!"

 What did Jesus do?
He said, "Go to the priests." The men weren't healed yet, but they obeyed. And as they went, their bodies were healed! The leprosy was gone!

 Did the 10 men come back and thank Jesus?
Only one man came back, thanking God for the miracle!

Thank God for your blessings today. If you are *healthy*, thank Him . . . many people are sick. If you have *food to eat*, thank Him . . . many people are hungry. Thank God every day for all the blessings He gives you!

hug! time

Give the one who is thankful . . . a great big *hug!*

♥ "I Want to See Jesus!"
Luke 19:1-10

Jesus came to seek
and save those
who are lost.
(Luke 19:10)

Crowds of people followed Jesus. A tax collector named Zacchaeus was there. He wanted to see Jesus. But he was too short to see over the crowd. Then he had an idea!

💜 **What did Zacchaeus do?**
There was a tall tree up ahead beside the road. So Zacchaeus climbed up the tree. As Jesus passed, He looked up at Zacchaeus and said, "Come down. I must stay at your house today!"

💜 **Did Zacchaeus change after he met Jesus?**
Yes, he did!

When Zacchaeus came down the tree, he was a *lost* person. That means he did not know about or believe in Jesus. But Jesus came to save the lost! He went to Zacchaeus's house and told him about God's plan. Zacchaeus believed and was *saved*!

hug!
time

💜
Give the one who wants to see Jesus . . . a great big hug!

♥ Do This to Remember
Luke 22

"Do this to remember me."
(Luke 22:19)

Jesus was having Passover dinner with His disciples. They ate a special meal to remember how God saved the Jews from slavery in Egypt. But Jesus knew this was a very special Passover.

What was special about this Passover?
Jesus used the Passover to teach His disciples why He had to go to the cross. He took the bread, gave thanks, and broke it. Jesus said, "This is my body, *broken* for you."

 What do we call this special meal?
It's called Communion.

Jesus said to do this to remember that He was broken and died for us. *Communion* means "common union." All Christians have something in common. We worship the One who was broken to save us from our sin.

hug!
time

Give the one who knows what *Communion* means . . . a great big

hug!

♥ He Is Risen!

Mark 16:1-7

"He is risen!"
(Luke 24:6)

It was just after sunrise on Sunday morning. Three women went to the place where Jesus was buried. Were they ever surprised! The big, heavy stone covering the entrance had been rolled away!

 What did they find inside?
As they entered the place where Jesus was buried, they were even more surprised! Jesus was not there! They saw an angel who told them, "Jesus isn't here! He is risen!"

 Was Jesus really alive?
Yes! The Bible says God raised Jesus from the dead!

Today Jesus lives in heaven. If we love Jesus, someday we will be there with Him. Jesus is stronger than death! Every year at Easter, we remember the day Jesus rose from the dead. That's why we say, *"He is risen!"*

hug! time

Give the one who can say, "He is risen!". . . a great big

hug!

♥ Stephen Forgives

Acts 6–7

"If you forgive those who sin against you, your heavenly Father will forgive you."

(Matthew 6:14)

Stephen served the Lord faithfully. He was full of God's love and grace. He told everyone about the love of Jesus. Stephen was a good man, but something very bad happened to him.

 What happened to Stephen?
Stephen got in trouble for doing the right thing. He told the truth when he said, "You people disobey God!" But this made the priests very angry. They threw rocks at Stephen and hurt him. Before Stephen went to heaven to be with Jesus, he forgave them.

Should we forgive people who hurt us?
Yes, just like Stephen did.

Stephen forgave because he wanted to obey Jesus and be like Him. Jesus said, "If you forgive those who hurt you, God will forgive you." So be like Stephen . . . and Jesus. Learn to forgive!

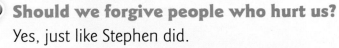

hug!
time

Give the one who is learning to forgive . . . a great big hug!

♥ Prepare to Share

Acts 8:26-38

Be a good worker . . . who correctly explains the word of truth.
(2 Timothy 2:15)

142

Philip was a disciple of Jesus. An angel appeared to him and told him where to go. On the way, Philip met a man from Ethiopia. He was sitting by the road, reading the Bible.

 What did Philip say to him?

Philip asked the man if he understood what he was reading. "I need a teacher," the man answered. Philip was *prepared to share!* He explained the Good News about Jesus! When they passed some water, Philip baptized the man.

How can I prepare to share?

Prepare to share by beginning with prayer!

Philip spent time with God each day. He read his Bible and memorized favorite verses too! Like Philip, we should *prepare to share* the very same way. Read your Bible and pray!

hug! time

Give the one who will *prepare to share* . . . a great big hug!

Changed on the Damascus Road

Acts 9:1-22

Let God transform you into a new person by changing the way you think.
(Romans 12:2)

Saul was walking on the road to Damascus. He was going there to look for followers of Jesus, called Christians. He wanted to catch them and put them in prison. Saul hated Christians! But God had a plan to change Saul's thinking.

 How did God change Saul?

On the way to Damascus, a bright light blinded Saul. He heard the voice of Jesus say, "Saul, why are you so mean to Me?" Saul was afraid! But when Jesus told him to go into the city, Saul obeyed.

 What happened next?

God sent a man to heal Saul's eyes. He could see again!

When his sight returned, Saul repented. That means he changed his way of thinking. Now he loved Jesus and wanted to help Christians, not hurt them. Saul started telling everyone that Jesus is Lord! When we accept Jesus as Lord, our thinking is changed . . . just like Saul's!

hug! time

Give the one whose life is changed by Jesus . . . a great big **hug!**

♥ It's a Miracle!

Acts 9:36-42

Remember the wonders
he has performed and
his miracles.
(Psalm 105:5)

Dorcas was a follower of Jesus. She was always doing kind things for others and helping the poor. She even made clothes for them. One day, Dorcas became very sick and died. Her friends were so sad. But they believed that prayer changes things!

❤ **Did they pray for Dorcas?**
Yes. Peter prayed and asked God for a *miracle*. Then he said, "Dorcas, get up." Dorcas opened her eyes and sat up! God made Dorcas alive again because of Peter's *miracle-prayer*!

❤ **Can my prayers change things?**
Prayer *always* changes things!

When we pray, God might change something big, like the miracle that saved Dorcas. Or He might change something not so big, like helping you sleep at night. Just remember, big or small, every prayer is a *miracle-prayer*!

hug! time

❤

Give the one who believes in miracles . . . a great big

hug!

147

♡ John Mark

Acts 12:25–13:5

"As for me and my
family, we will serve
the LORD."
(Joshua 24:15)

John Mark had a special friend named Peter. Peter was one of the 12 disciples who followed Jesus. When Peter was put into prison for preaching, John Mark came to serve.

How did he serve?

John Mark sat outside the prison and listened to Peter. Then he wrote down many wonderful stories about Jesus. You can read these writings in the Bible book of Mark!

How can I serve the Lord?

There are lots of ways to serve!

John Mark served God by writing. Maybe you will use your hands to help others. Or maybe you will use your voice to praise God. Joshua said you must *choose* whom you will serve. We should always choose to serve the Lord!

hug!
time

Give the one who chooses to serve the Lord . . . a great big

hug!

♥ The Prison Shakes!

Acts 16:16-34

Saul's whole life was changed by Jesus. He even changed his name to Paul. But some people did not like Paul's preaching. They put Paul and his friend Silas in prison for telling others about Jesus.

What happened in the prison?
Paul and Silas were singing praise songs to God. Suddenly, an earthquake shook the prison. The jailer thought they had escaped until Paul shouted, "We are here!" The jailer cried out, "How can I be saved, like you?"

 How did Paul answer the jailer?
Paul said, "Believe and accept what Jesus has done for you. Then you will be saved."

What did Jesus do for you? He died on the cross to take away your sins. When you believe this, you are saved!

hug!
time

Give the one who is saved by Jesus . . . a great big hug!

♥ Love in Action

Acts 17:1-9

Let's not merely say that we love each other; let us show the truth by our actions.
(1 John 3:18)

Jason's house was a place where God's people were welcome. His missionary friends, Paul and Silas, were coming to visit. But some mean men wanted to put Paul and Silas in prison. So they came to Jason's house with a crowd of angry people.

 What happened next?
Paul and Silas weren't there, so the crowd took Jason and some other believers instead. Then they brought Jason before a judge. They called Jason a troublemaker because he told people about Jesus. But God protected him. Jason put his love for the Lord into action!

Can I put my love for the Lord into action?
Yes, you can!

Love is an action word. It's something we *do*, not something we only talk about. The Bible says love is being *patient* and *kind* to others. When we put our love into action like that, God is pleased!

hug! time

Give the one who puts love into action . . . a great big hug!

♥ Serve Jesus by Serving Others

Romans 16:1-2

"When you did it to one of the least of these my brothers and sisters, you were doing it to me!"

(Matthew 25:40)

154

We hear about Phoebe only once in the Bible. Paul said she was a servant of Jesus and someone who should be honored. In her home church, Phoebe was known for her good deeds!

 What made her a good servant?
More than anything, Phoebe wanted to serve Jesus! She learned to do that by serving, loving, and helping others. Jesus said that when we do something kind for others, it is the same as doing it for Him!

Can I serve Jesus the same way?
Yes, you can!

When you see someone who is hungry or thirsty or sick, help that person as if you were helping Jesus. Everyone matters to Jesus. He wants us to take care of people who need help. Serve others as Phoebe did, and you serve Jesus!

hug! time

Give the one who serves Jesus by serving others . . . a great big

hug!

♥ Love One Another

2 John 1:4-6

Let us continue to love
one another, for love
comes from God.
(1 John 4:7)

There are 20 "one another" commands found in the Bible. God says we should serve *one another*, encourage *one another*, and forgive *one another*. But one of these "one another" commands appears more than the rest.

♥ **Which "one another" is it?**
LOVE *one another*! Since God *is* love, He wants us to love *one another*. It's our job to share God's love with everyone!

♥ **How can I show God's love to others?**
The Bible says that love does no wrong to others. That means we should never hurt anyone or say mean things. Instead, we should be patient and kind. We should say nice things and be helpful. Remember, God gives us the love, patience, kindness, and goodness that we can share with *one another*!

hug! time

♥

Give the one who loves others . . . a great big

hug!

Heavenly Hugs!

Heaven must be full of hugs. Why? Because the Bible says "God is love!"
And where the spirit of love is, you'll always find lots of hugs!
God wants us to love Him too! All the Bible characters we read about in
this book loved God with all their heart! And I know *you* love God too!

Let's tell Him so in a prayer right now!

**Dear God,
You are wonderful! I wish I could give You a
great big hug right now. One day I will!
I love You, Lord, and I know You love me, too!
Remember, I'm saving a great big
heavenly hug just for You.
Until I see You, I will love You in my heart.**

Hugs forever!

Sign your name here:

share·a·hug!™

www.share-a-hug.com